Acknowledgement

Special thanks to Dr. Shary Maskel, Executive Director of The Hill Center from 1985-2014; veteran faculty member, Shauna Saunders; Outreach Coordinator, Pam Hoggard; and all of the Hill trainers, faculty, and staff who contributed to the development of the Hill Readers.

© 2017 The Hill Center, Inc. All Rights Reserved.

No part of this book may be reproduced, in any form or by any means, electronic or mechanical—including but not limited to—photocopy, recording, or any information storage and retrieval system, without written permission from the publisher.

Use of this book is restricted by a licensing agreement.

Requests for permission to make copies of any part of this work should be addressed to: The Hill Center, 3200 Pickett Road, Durham, NC 27705.

"The Hill Center Program" and "The Hill Center" are trademarks of The Hill Center, Inc.

Hill Readers
Book 1

Written by Sharon P. Maskel, Ed.D.

Hill Reading Level: **K**
Flesch-Kincaid Reading Level: **Kindergarten**

Hill Reading Level

The Hill Reading Level is aligned with the Word Attack sequence of the Hill Reading Achievement Program (HillRAP), and the Common Core State Standards. The Flesch-Kincaid Grade Level Readability Formula has been assigned to each book to provide a grade level equivalency.

Source: The Flesch-Kincaid Grade Level Readability Formula
http://www.readabilityformulas.com/free-readability-formula-tests.php

Hill Readers—Book 1
Table of Contents

Chapter 1

WAT 004 Short Vowels in Isolation (a)
         VC a Word Families (at)
         CVC a Words by Families (bat)

WAT 005 CVC a Words (mad)

SWD 001 Sight Words

1a "The Cat" 1
1b "The Fat Cat" 3
1c "The Cat Sat" 5
1d "Pat the Cat" 7
1e "The Hat on the Cat" 9
1f "Pat the Hat on the Cat" 11
1g "The Bat" 13
1h "Pat the Fat Cat" 15
1i "The Cat and the Rat" 17
1j "Pat the Rat and the Cat" 19

Hill Readers—Book 1
Table of Contents (cont'd)

Chapter 2

WAT 004   *Short Vowels in Isolation (a)*
                    VC a Word Families (at)
                    CVC a Words by Families (bat)

WAT 005   *CVC a Words (mad)*

SWD 001   *Sight Words*

2a	"Pat the Rat"	21
2b	"Cat on the Mat"	23
2c	"Sad Cat"	25
2d	"Dad on the Mat"	27
2e	"Sad Cat"	29
2f	"Dad is Mad"	31
2g	"The Pad on the Mat"	33
2h	"Dad's Hat"	35
2i	"Tad and the Cat"	37
2j	"Tad Bats"	39

Hill Readers—Book 1
Table of Contents (cont'd)

Chapter 3

WAT 004   Short Vowels in Isolation (a)
                VC a Word Families (at)
                CVC a Words by Families (bat)

WAT 005   CVC a Words (mad)

SWD 001   Sight Words

3a	"Cat on a Lap"	41
3b	"Mad Dad"	43
3c	"The Cat and Rat Nap"	45
3d	"Tad's Hat"	47
3e	"Tad Had a Cap"	49
3f	"Tad at Bat"	51
3g	"Tap the Cat"	53
3h	"The Cat Naps"	55
3i	"Dad Had a Map"	57
3j	"Tad Bats with His Cap"	59

Hill Readers—Book 1
Table of Contents (cont'd)

Chapter 4

WAT 004   *Short Vowels in Isolation (a)*
                 VC a Word Families (at)
                 CVC a Words by Families (bat)

WAT 005   *CVC a Words (mad)*

SWD 001   *Sight Words*

4a	"Cap in the Bag"	61
4b	"The Map"	63
4c	"A Rag in a Bag"	65
4d	"Tad's Rag Hat"	67
4e	"Tad Tags the Mat"	69
4f	"Tad's Nap"	71

Hill Readers—Book 1
Table of Contents (cont'd)

Chapter 5

WAT 004   Short Vowels in Isolation (a)
VC a Word Families (at)
CVC a Words by Families (bat)

WAT 005   CVC a Words (mad)

SWD 001   Sight Words

5a   "Babs the Cat" 73
5b   "Babs on the Mat" 75
5c   "The Mad Rat" 77
5d   "Nab the Rat" 79
5e   "Dad's Cab" 81
5f   "A Map in the Yellow Cab" 83
5g   "Pat the Lab" 85
5h   "The Lab in the Cab" 87

Hill Readers—Book 1
Table of Contents (cont'd)

Chapter 6

WAT 004   *Short Vowels in Isolation (a)*
VC a Word Families (at)
CVC a Words by Families (bat)

WAT 005   *CVC a Words (mad)*

SWD 001   *Sight Words*

6a   "Max's Nap" 89
6b   "Max's Bag" 91
6c   "Wax for the Yellow Cab" 93
6d   "Wax the Cab" 95

Hill Readers—Book 1
Table of Contents (cont'd)

Chapter 7

WAT 004   *Short Vowels in Isolation (a)*
                VC a Word Families (at)
                CVC a Words by Families (bat)

WAT 005   *CVC a Words (mad)*

SWD 001   *Sight Words*

7a   "Pals" 97
7b   "Caps with Maps" 99
7c   "Sal's Yellow Hat" 101

Hill Readers—Book 1
Table of Contents (cont'd)

Chapter 8

WAT 004 — Short Vowels in Isolation (a)
VC a Word Families (at)
CVC a Words by Families (bat)

WAT 005 — CVC a Words (mad)

SWD 001 — Sight Words

8a	"Dan's Tan Van"	103
8b	"Dan's Map"	105
8c	"Max Tags the Bag"	107
8d	"Babs Naps"	109
8e	"Ham and Yams for Hal"	111
8f	"The Rat in the Pan"	113
8g	"The Fan in the Cab"	115
8h	"Wax the Tan Van"	117

Hill Readers—Book 1
Table of Contents (cont'd)

Chapter 9

WAT 004   Short Vowels in Isolation (a)
                 VC a Word Families (at)
                 CVC a Words by Families (bat)

WAT 005   CVC a Words (mad)

SWD 001   Sight Words

9a	"Ham and Yams"	119
9b	"Max's Ham"	121
9c	"Jam in Dan's Van"	123
9d	"Yams in a Bag"	125
9e	"Rags for Pam"	127
9f	"You Can Tag Pam"	129

Hill Readers—Book 1
Table of Contents (cont'd)

Review Words.. 131
Review Sight Words.................................. 132

"The Cat"

cat	sat	the

The cat sat.

Comprehension Questions

"The Cat"

1. The cat ___.

2. Where do you think the cat sat?

"The Fat Cat"

fat

The fat cat sat.

Comprehension Questions 1-1b

"The Fat Cat"

1. Why do you think the cat is fat?

2. What else could be fat?

"The Cat Sat"

The cat sat.

The cat sat on the mat.

On the mat the cat sat.

The fat cat sat on the mat.

Comprehension Questions 1-1c

"The Cat Sat"

1. The cat sat on the ___.

2. What kind of mat do you think the cat sat on?
    a. a placemat
    b. a soft mat
    c. a door mat
    d. a bath mat

3. Why do you think the cat sat there?

4. Draw the cat on the mat.

"Pat the Cat"

$$\boxed{\text{pat}}$$

Pat the cat.

Pat the cat on the mat.

On the mat the fat cat sat.

The fat cat sat on the mat.

Pat the fat cat on the mat.

Comprehension Questions

"Pat the Cat"

1. What should you do to the cat?

2. How do you think the cat feels when you pet him?

3. What is another word for **pat** in the story?

4. What is the opposite of **fat**?
    a. chubby
    b. tall
    c. thin
    d. short

"The Hat on the Cat"

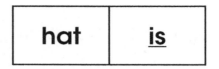

The hat is on the cat.

The cat is on the mat.

The hat is on the cat on the mat.

Comprehension Questions 1-1e

"The Hat on the Cat"

1. The hat is on the ___ .

2. Where is the cat?

3. Why do you think the cat is wearing a hat?

4. Name a type of **hat**.

5. Draw the cat wearing a hat.

"Pat the Hat on the Cat"

Pat the fat cat.

Pat the fat cat on the mat.

On the cat is a hat.

Pat the hat on the cat.

The hat is on the fat cat on the mat.

Comprehension Questions

"Pat the Hat on the Cat"

1. Where is the hat?

2. The cat is on the ___.

3. What word tells about the cat?

4. Draw the fat cat on the mat wearing a hat.

"The Bat"

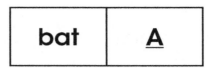

A bat is on the mat.

A fat bat is on the mat.

Pat the bat on the mat.

Comprehension Questions

"The Bat"

1. The bat is on the ___.

2. What does the batter do in this story?

3. What game is being played?

4. What is the mat for?

5. What is another kind of **bat**?

6. Draw a bat.

"Pat the Fat Cat"

The cat is on the mat.

The fat cat sat on the mat.

Bat at the fat cat on the mat.

Pat the fat cat on the mat.

Comprehension Questions

"Pat the Fat Cat"

1. The ___ is on the mat.
2. The fat cat ___ on the mat.
3. Who might bat at the cat?
   a. a mouse
   b. a dog
   c. a fish
   d. a cow
4. Who might pat the cat?
5. What do you think the cat will do if you bat at it?
6. What does **bat** mean in this story?
   a. sports equipment
   b. animal
   c. hit
   d. feelings

"The Cat and the Rat"

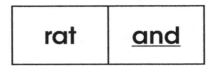

The cat and the rat sat.

The cat and the rat sat on the mat.

The cat and the rat sat on the hat.

The cat and the rat sat on the hat on the mat.

Comprehension Questions

"The Cat and the Rat"

1. The cat and the rat sat on the ___.

2. Who are the **characters** in this story?

3. What is the **problem** in this story?

4. What might happen to the hat?

5. Do you think this story is real? Why or why not?

6. Draw a picture of what is happening in this story.

"Pat the Rat and the Cat"

Pat the rat.

Pat the fat cat.

Pat the rat and the fat cat.

Pat the rat and the fat cat on the mat.

Comprehension Questions 1-1j

"Pat the Rat and the Cat"

1. Pat the ___ and the ___ ___.

2. What does the cat look like?

3. Why would you pat a rat? Why or why not?

4. What animal is like a rat?

5. What is another word for pat in this story?

"Pat the Rat"

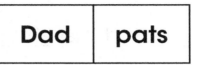

Pat the rat, Dad.

Pat the rat on the mat.

Dad pats the rat on the mat.

Comprehension Questions

"Pat the Rat"

1. ___ pats the rat.

2. Who are the **characters** in this story?

3. Why would Dad pat a rat?

4. Why might the rat be on a mat?

5. What is a **mat** in this story?

"Cat on the Mat"

had

The cat had a mat.

The cat sat on the mat.

Dad pats the cat.

Dad pats the cat on the mat.

Comprehension Questions 1-2b

"Cat on the Mat"

1. Dad ___ the cat.

2. Who are the **characters** in this story?

3. What kind of a mat do you think the cat had?

4. How do you think the cat feels?

5. What might the cat do next?

"Sad Cat"

> sad

The cat is sad.

Dad pats the cat.

Dad pats the sad cat.

Pat the sad cat, Dad.

Comprehension Questions

"Sad Cat"

1. ___ ___ is sad.

2. Who are the **characters** in this story?

3. Why do you think Dad pats the cat?

4. How would the cat feel then?

5. Who do you think is telling Dad to pat the cat?

6. Draw the sad cat.

"Dad on the Mat"

Dad sat on the mat.

Dad sat on the mat with the cat.

Pat the cat on the mat, Dad.

Dad pats the cat on the mat.

Comprehension Questions 1-2d

"Dad on the Mat"

1. ___ is on the mat.

2. Who are the **characters** in this story?

3. Why do you think Dad pats the cat?

"Sad Cat"

The cat is sad.

Pat the sad cat.

Pat the sad cat on the mat.

The sad cat is on the mat.

Comprehension Questions

"Sad Cat"

1. How does the cat feel?

2. Who is the **character** in this story?

3. What might make the cat sad?

4. What is another word for **sad**?

"Dad is Mad"

mad	bad

Dad is mad.

The cat sat on the hat.

The bad cat sat on Dad's hat.

Pat sad Dad.

Comprehension Questions

"Dad is Mad"

1. Who are the **characters** in this story?

2. What is the **problem** in this story?

3. Do you think the cat in this story is bad? Why or why not?

4. Who might pat Dad?

5. Do you think this will make Dad feel better?

6. What is another word for **bad**?

"The Pad on the Mat"

pad

The pad is on the mat.

The cat sat on the pad.

The cat sat on the pad on the mat.

The cat is on the mat on the pad.

Comprehension Questions

"The Pad on the Mat"

1. The ___ is on the mat.

2. Where is the cat in this story?

3. Draw a picture of the cat, the pad, and the mat.

"Dad's Hat"

> Dad's

Dad's hat is on the cat.

Pat Dad's hat.

Pat Dad's hat on the cat.

Pat Dad's hat on the cat on the mat.

Comprehension Questions

"Dad's Hat"

1. What kind of hat do you think it is?

2. Why do you think the hat is on the cat?

3. Why would you pat the hat?

4. Draw a picture of the cat, the hat, and the mat.

"Tad and the Cat"

| Tad |

The cat is sad.

Tad pats the cat.

The cat is on the mat.

Tad and the cat sat on the mat.

Comprehension Questions

"Tad and the Cat"

1. Tad and the cat sat on the ___.

2. Who are the **characters** in this story?

3. Why might the cat be sad?

4. Why might Tad pat the cat?

"Tad Bats"

Tad bats at the cat.

Tad bats at the cat on the mat.

Bat the cat, Dad.

Tad and Dad bat at the cat.

Comprehension Questions

"Tad Bats"

1. Tad ___ at the cat.

2. Who are the **characters** in this story?

3. Who might be telling Dad, "Bat the cat?"

4. Why do you think Tad and Dad bat at the cat?

5. What does **bat** mean in this story?
   a. hits
   b. sports equipment
   c. flying animal
   d. catches

"Cat on a Lap"

Dad is on the mat.

The cat is on Dad's lap.

The cat sat on his lap.

Pat the cat on his lap.

Pat the cat on Dad's lap on the mat.

Comprehension Questions 1-3a

"Cat on a Lap"

1. ___ the cat on his lap.

2. Who are the **characters** in this story?

3. Where do you think this story takes place?

4. Why do you think the cat is on Dad's lap?

5. What might the cat do after you pat it?

6. What is a **lap** in this story?
   a. a sip
   b. the distance across a pool
   c. the place your legs form when you sit down
   d. travel around a track

"Mad Dad"

The cat sat on Dad's hat.

Dad is mad at the cat.

The cat is sad.

Pat the sad cat, Dad.

The sad cat sat on his mat.

Comprehension Questions

"Mad Dad"

1. The cat ___ on Dad's hat.

2. How did Dad feel?

3. Who are the **characters** in this story?

4. Why do you think the cat is sad?

5. Why should Dad pat the cat?

6. Why might the cat sit on his mat?

7. What else might a cat do that is bad?

"The Cat and Rat Nap"

nap

The cat sat on Dad's lap.

The cat had a nap on Dad's lap.

The rat had a nap on the pad.

The cat and the rat had a nap.

The cat and the rat had a nap on the pad.

Comprehension Questions 1-3c

"The Cat and Rat Nap"

1. The rat had a nap on the ___.

2. Where did the cat nap first? Second?

3. Who are the **characters** in this story?

4. Why do you think the cat napped on Dad's lap?

5. What is a **pad** in this story?
   a. a place to live
   b. a soft material
   c. a tablet of paper
   d. a place to park a car

"Tad's Hat"

Tad's

Tad sat on his mat.

Tad had a nap on his mat.

Tad sat on his mat and had a nap.

Tad's hat is on his mat.

Tad had a nap on his mat with his hat.

Comprehension Questions

"Tad's Hat"

1. Tad's ___ is on his mat.

2. What did Tad do first?

3. What did Tad do next?

4. Who do you think Tad is?

5. How do you think Tad felt? Why?

6. Why do think Tad had a nap on his hat?

7. What is another word for **nap**?

"Tad Had a Cap"

cap

Tad had a cap.

The cap is on his lap.

The cat sat on Tad's cap on his lap.

Tad's cap is on his lap.

Comprehension Questions

"Tad Had a Cap"

1. What did Tad have?

2. The cat sat on Tad's ___ on his ___.

3. Who are the **characters** in this story?

4. Why do you think the cat sat on Tad's cap?

5. How do you think Tad's cap looked at the end of the story?

6. What is the **cap** in this story?
   a. a lid
   b. a gun
   c. a hat
   d. limit

"Tad at Bat"

was

Tad was at bat.

Tad had his cap.

His bat is at the mat.

Tad bats at the mat.

Tad bats at the mat with his cap on.

Comprehension Questions

"Tad at Bat"

1. What does Tad do with his bat in this story?

2. Where does this story take place?

3. Why did Tad have a cap?

4. What game is Tad playing?

5. What do you think will happen next?

"Tap the Cat"

tap	he

The fat cat naps on Tad's lap.

Tap the fat cat on his lap.

Tad taps the fat cat on his lap.

He taps and pats the fat cat on his lap.

Comprehension Questions 1-3g

"Tap the Cat"

1. Where is the cat?

2. What word tells about the cat?

3. Tad ___ and ___ the fat cat on his lap.

4. Who are the **characters** in this story?

"The Cat Naps"

The cat on the mat sat on Dad's lap.

Dad taps the cat.

He taps the cat on his lap.

The cat naps on his lap.

Comprehension Questions

"The Cat Naps"

1. Where is the cat?

2. Dad ___ the cat.

3. Who are the **characters** in this story?

4. What did the cat do at the end of the story?

"Dad Had a Map"

> map

Dad had a map.

He had the map on his lap.

He taps the map on his lap.

The map is on his lap.

Comprehension Questions

"Dad Had a Map"

1. Where do you think the story takes place?

2. Why might Dad need a map?

3. Why might Dad tap the map?

4. Name a place you could use a map to find.

5. What does **tap** mean in this story?
   a. tear
   b. hit lightly
   c. dance
   d. spell

6. What is a map of the world that is shaped like a ball called?

1-3j

"Tad Bats with His Cap"

Dad had a cap for Tad.

He had the cap for Tad.

Tad bats with his cap on.

At the mat, Tad bats.

He bats with his cap on.

Comprehension Questions　　　1-3j

"Tad Bats with His Cap"

1. Dad had a ___ for Tad.

2. Who are the **characters** in this story?

3. Where do you think this story takes place?

4. Why might Tad need a cap?

5. What is a **mat** in this story?
   a. a placemat
   b. a doormat
   c. a base
   d. a rug

"Cap in the Bag"

$$\boxed{\text{bag}}$$

Tad had the cap in the bag.

His cap was in the bag.

He sat on the mat with his bag.

He had a nap with his cap on his lap.

Comprehension Questions 1-4a

"Cap in the Bag"

1. What did Tad have?

2. Where was Tad's cap?

3. He sat ___ ___ ___ with his bag.

4. Who is the **character** in this story?

5. Why might Tad have a nap?

6. What might a bag be made of?

"The Map"

The map was on Dad's lap.

He had a nap with the map on his lap.

Is the map on his lap?

Is the map on the mat?

The map is on his lap.

Comprehension Questions

"The Map"

1. Who is the **character** in this story?

2. How do you think Dad felt at the beginning of the story? What words make you think this?

3. Where do you think Dad might be sitting?

"A Rag in a Bag"

rag

Dad had a rag.

He had the rag in a bag.

The bag is on the mat.

The rag is in the bag on the mat.

Comprehension Questions 1-4c

"A Rag in a Bag"

1. Dad had a ___.

2. Where was the rag?

3. Who is the **character** in this story?

4. What is a **rag** in this story?
   a. music
   b. a piece of cloth
   c. a piece of paper
   d. a plant

"Tad's Rag Hat"

Tad had a rag.

The rag is Tad's hat.

Is the rag a hat?

Is the rag a cap?

The rag is Tad's hat.

Tad had a rag hat.

Comprehension Questions

"Tad's Rag Hat"

1. The ___ is Tad's hat.

2. Who is the **character** in this story?

3. How do you think Tad's hat might feel? Why?

4. Draw a picture of Tad's rag hat.

"Tad Tags the Mat"

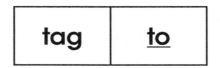

Tad, tag the mat.

Tag the mat, Tad.

He tags the mat and pats his bat.

Tad had to tag the mat.

He bats and tags the mat.

Comprehension Questions

"Tad Tags the Mat"

1. What should Tad do?
2. Who is the **character** in this story?
3. What game is Tad playing?
4. What position is Tad playing?
   a. catcher
   b. pitcher
   c. batter
   d. coach
5. What will Tad do **after** he bats?
6. What does **tag** mean in this story?
   a. a label for clothing
   b. to touch
   c. to run
   d. to mark
7. What is the **mat** in this story?
   a. a doormat
   b. a base
   c. a placemat
   d. a rug

"Tad's Nap"

Dad nags Tad.

Tad had to nap.

He had to nap.

He had to nap on Dad's lap.

He was sad.

Pat sad Tad on Dad's lap.

Tad naps.

Comprehension Questions

"Tad's Nap"

1. Who had to nap?

2. Where did Tad nap?

3. Who are the **characters** in this story?

4. Where to do you think Dad naps?

5. Why do you think Tad was sad?

6. What does **nags** mean in this story?
   a. bothers
   b. horses
   c. sings to
   d. helps

"Babs the Cat"

$$\boxed{\textbf{Babs}}$$

Babs is Tad's cat.

Pat Babs the cat.

Babs naps.

Babs naps on Tad's lap.

Comprehension Questions

"Babs the Cat"

1. ___ is Tad's cat.

2. What should you do to Babs?

3. What does Babs do in this story?

4. Who are the **characters** in this story?

5. How do you think Babs feels at the end of this story?

"Babs on the Mat"

Babs sat on the mat.

Dad pats Babs on the mat.

He pats Babs on the mat.

Babs naps on the mat.

Comprehension Questions 1-5b

"Babs on the Mat"

1. Where was Babs?

2. Dad ___ Babs on the mat.

3. Who are the **characters** in this story?

4. Why do you think Babs naps on the mat?

"The Mad Rat"

The rat sat on the mat.

Pat the rat, Tad.

Tad pats the rat on the mat.

Is the rat mad, Tad?

The rat is mad.

Comprehension Questions

"The Mad Rat"

1. Where is the rat?

2. What should Tad do to the rat?

3. Who are the **characters** in this story?

4. Why might the rat be mad?

"Nab the Rat"

nab	in

The rat on the mat is mad.

Nab the rat, Tad.

The rat is mad.

Tad nabs the rat.

Is the rat in the bag?

The rat is in the bag.

Tad had the rat in the bag.

Comprehension Questions

"Nab the Rat"

1. What should Tad do to the rat?

2. How does the rat feel?

3. Who are the **characters** in this story?

4. Where is the rat at the **beginning** of this story?

5. Where is the rat at the **end** of this story?

6. What does **nab** mean in this story?

"Dad's Cab"

cab	yellow

Dad had a cab.

The cab is yellow.

Dad had a yellow cab.

He had a nap in his cab.

Dad had a nap in his yellow cab.

Comprehension Questions

"Dad's Cab"

1. Dad had a ___.

2. What color is Dad's cab?

3. What did Dad do in his cab?

4. Who is the **character** in this story?

5. What is a **cab** in this story?

"A Map in the Yellow Cab"

Dad had a map.

He had a map in his cab.

Is the map on his lap?

Dad had a map on his lap in his cab.

Dad had a map on his lap in his yellow cab.

Comprehension Questions

"A Map in the Yellow Cab"

1. What did Dad have?

2. Where is the map?

3. Who is the **character** in this story?

4. Where does this story take place? (What is the **setting**?)

5. Why might Dad have a map on his lap?

6. What is the one place you might use a map to get to?

"Pat the Lab"

| Lab |

The Lab sat on the mat.

Pat the Lab, Tad.

Tad pats the Lab on the mat.

The Lab wags.

The Lab sat on Tad's lap.

Pat the Lab, Tad.

Tad pats the Lab on his lap.

The Lab wags.

Comprehension Questions

"Pat the Lab"

1. Who are the **characters** in this story?

2. Where is the Lab in the **beginning** of this story?

3. Where is the Lab at the **end** of the story?

4. Why do you think the Lab is in Tad's lap?

5. Why do you think the Lab wags?

6. What is another animal that wags?

7. What does **wags** mean in this story?

8. What is the **Lab** in this story?

"The Lab in the Cab"

Dad had the Lab in the cab.

Is the Lab in the cab with Dad?

The Lab is in the cab with Dad.

The Lab sat on the mat in the cab.

He sat on Dad's lap in the cab.

The Lab had a nap on Dad's lap.

He had a nap on Dad's lap on the mat in the cab.

The Lab naps in the cab.

Comprehension Questions 1-5h

"The Lab in the Cab"

1. Where was the Lab?

2. What did the Lab do?

3. Who are the **characters** in this story?

4. Where does this story take place? (What is the **setting**?)

5. Why might the Lab be in the cab?

6. Do you think a cab is a good place to take a nap? Why or why not?

"Max's Nap"

Max

Max is a Lab.

Max the Lab had a nap.

He had a nap in Dad's cab.

Is Max in the cab with Dad?

Max is in the cab with Dad.

Max had a nap in Dad's yellow cab.

Max had a nap on the mat in Dad's yellow cab.

Max the Lab had a nap in Dad's yellow cab.

Comprehension Questions　　　　　　1-6a

"Max's Nap"

1. Who is Max?

2. Who are the **characters** in this story?

3. Where does this story take place? (What is the **setting**?)

4. Why might Max take a nap in the cab?

5. What do you think Dad's job might be?

"Max's Bag"

Tad had a bag for Max.

The bag was yellow.

He had a yellow bag for Max.

Max had a nap on the bag.

He had a nap on the yellow bag.

The bag is a rag!

Comprehension Questions

"Max's Bag"

1. What did Tad have for Max?

2. What did Max do with the bag?

3. Who are the **characters** in this story?

4. How do you think the bag became a rag?

5. Why do you think Max had a nap on the bag?

6. What do you think might be in the bag?

"Wax for the Yellow Cab"

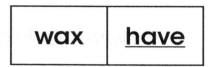

Dad's cab is bad.

The cab had to have wax.

Tad had to wax the cab for Dad.

He had wax for Dad's yellow cab.

The wax is in the pad.

Tad had to wax the yellow cab.

Comprehension Questions 1-6c

"Wax for the Yellow Cab"

1. The cab had to have ___.

2. Who had to wax the cab?

3. Who is the **character** in this story?

4. What does **bad** mean in this story?
   a. dirty
   b. not behaving
   c. sad
   d. mad

5. What is **wax** in this story?
   a. a candle
   b. a polish
   c. water
   d. food

6. What would a **pad** be used for in this story?

"Wax the Cab"

Tad had to wax the cab.

He had to wax the yellow cab for Dad.

The yellow cab is bad.

Tad had a pad to wax the cab.

He had a rag to wax the cab.

He had a pad and a rag to wax the cab.

Tad had to wax the yellow cab with his pad and his rag.

Comprehension Questions 1-6d

"Wax the Cab"

1. What was Tad's job?

2. What is wrong with the cab?

3. What color is the cab?

4. What did Tad use to wax the cab?

5. Who is the **character** in this story?

6. How do you think the yellow cab looks at the **end** of the story?

7. What is something that might need to be waxed?

"Pals"

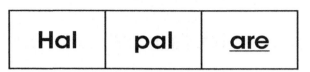

Hal is Tad's pal.

Tad is Hal's pal.

Hal and Tad are pals.

Hal and Tad bat at the mat.

Hal tags Tad at the mat.

Tad tags Hal at the mat.

Comprehension Questions 1-7a

"Pals"

1. Hal and Tad are ___.

2. Who are the **characters** in this story?

3. What is a **pal**?
    a. a dog
    b. a friend
    c. a player
    d. a plant

"Caps with Maps"

Tad and Hal have caps.

Tad and Hal have yellow caps.

The caps are rad!

Pat the caps, Tad.

Pat the caps, Hal.

Tad and Hal pat the caps.

Comprehension Questions 1-7b

"Caps with Maps"

1. What do Tad and Hal have?

2. What color are the caps?

3. Who are the **characters** in this story?

4. Why might Tad and Hal pat the caps?

5. What do you think **rad** means in the story?
    a. radical/cool
    b. red
    c. alive
    d. boring

"Sal's Yellow Hat"

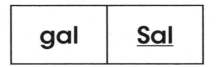

Sal is a gal.

Sal is Hal's pal.

Sal and Hal are pals.

Sal had a yellow hat.

Comprehension Questions 1-7c

"Sal's Yellow Hat"

1. What did Sal have?

2. Where is Sal's hat?

3. Who is the **character** in this story?

4. What is something that pals might do together?

5. What is a **pal** in this story?

6. What is a **gal** in this story?
   a. a boy
   b. a girl
   c. a cap
   d. a cat

"Dan's Tan Van"

Dan	van	man	tan

Dan is a man.

He had a van.

His van was tan.

Dan sat in his van.

He had a nap in his van.

Dan had a nap in his tan van.

Comprehension Questions

"Dan's Tan Van"

1. What color is Dan's van?

2. What did Dan do in his van?

3. Who is the **character** in this story?

4. Why do you think he did this?

5. What else might Dan do in his van?

"Dan's Map"

Dan's tan van had a map.

The map was in a bag in the van.

He had a map in his tan van.

Dan had the map on his lap.

He had the map on his lap in the tan van.

Dan had the map on his lap in the tan van.

Comprehension Questions 1-8b

"Dan's Map"

1. Who is the **character** in this story?

2. Where does this story take place (What is the **setting**?)

3. Where is the map in the **beginning** of the story?

4. Where is the map at the **end** of the story?

5. Why might the map be on Dan's lap?

6. Where do you think Dan might be going?

"Max Tags the Bag"

ran	can

Max the Lab ran.

He ran and ran.

Max can tag the bag.

Max tags the bag.

Tag the bag, Max.

Max tags the bag.

Max the Lab tags the bag.

Comprehension Questions   1-8c

"Max Tags the Bag"

1. What is Max doing?
2. Who is the **character** in this story?
3. Where does this story take place (What is the **setting**?)
4. How do you think the bag became a rag?
5. What does **tag** mean in this story?
   a. a label
   b. bite
   c. touch or tap
   d. pull
6. What do you think a **bag** is in this story?
   a. a lunch bag
   b. a base
   c. a grocery bag

"Babs Naps"

Babs the cat ran.

Babs ran with Max the Lab.

Babs and Max ran and ran.

Babs naps.

Babs can nap on the mat.

Babs the cat naps on the tan mat.

Pat Babs on the mat.

Babs naps on the tan mat.

Comprehension Questions 1-8d

"Babs Naps"

1. What did Babs and Max do?

2. What should you do to Babs?

3. Who are the **characters** in this story?

4. Why do you think Babs and Max ran and ran?

5. What do you think Max is doing while Babs sleeps?

"Ham and Yams for Hal"

Hal had a bag.

In the bag was ham.

Hal can have the ham in the pan.

Hal had ham in the pan.

Hal can have ham with yams.

He had yams and ham in his pan.

It was ham and yams for Hal.

He had yams and ham on the mat.

Comprehension Questions   1-8e

"Ham and Yams for Hal"

1. What was in the bag?

2. Who is the **character** in this story?

3. Why did Hal put the ham in the pan?

4. Do you like ham and yams? Why or why not?

5. What else might you eat with ham?

6. What are **yams**?
   a. meat
   b. dessert
   c. sweet potatoes
   d. candy

7. What kind of **mat** is in the story?
   a. a base
   b. a placemat
   c. a doormat
   d. a person

"The Rat in the Pan"

Tad ran to the van with a pan.

In the pan was a rat.

Tad had to nab the rat.

It was in the pan.

It was a bad rat.

He had a bad rat in the pan.

Tad was mad at the bad rat.

Tad had the bad rat in the pan.

Comprehension Questions

"The Rat in the Pan"

1. What is in the pan?

2. Who are the **characters** in this story?

3. Where does the story take place? (What is the **setting**?)

4. Why do you think Tad was mad?

5. What should be in a pan?

6. What might you do if you found a rat in your pan?

7. What does **nab** mean in this story?
   a. catch
   b. a cracker
   c. hit
   d. steal

"The Fan in the Cab"

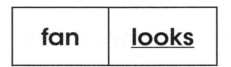

Dad had a fan for his cab.

He had a fan for his yellow cab.

The fan ran and ran.

It ran in the cab.

The fan sat on the mat in the cab.

It looks bad in the cab

The cab looks bad with the fan in it.

The cab looks bad with the fan on the mat.

Comprehension Questions 1-8g

"The Fan in the Cab"

1. Who is the **character** in this story?

2. Where does this story take place? (What is the **setting**?)

3. Why do you think Dad had a fan in his cab?

4. What do you think Dad will do because his fan looks bad in the cab?

5. What is a **cab** in this story?
    a. a taxi
    b. the front part of a truck
    c. a cabin

6. What does **ran** mean in this story?

"Wax the Tan Van"

Dan's tan van looks bad.

Dan's tan van had to have a wax.

The wax was in the van in a pan.

The pan with the wax was in Dan's tan van.

Wax the van, Dan.

Dan can wax the van.

He can wax the van with a rag.

Dan had to wax his tan van with a rag.

Comprehension Questions 1-8h

"Wax the Tan Van"

1. Why did Dan's van look bad?

2. Who is the **character** in this story?

3. Where is the **setting** of this story?

4. Why do you think the wax was in the pan?

5. Why did Dan need a rag to wax his van?

6. What does wax do to a van or car?

7. What is a **rag** in this story?
   a. ripped fabric
   b. an old cloth
   c. a head wrap

"Ham and Yams"

ham	yams	they

The ham was in the bag.

The yams are in the pan.

Dad and Tad have ham and yams.

They have ham and yams on the mat.

Dad and Tad had to have naps.

Dad and Tad had naps.

They had ham and yams.

They had to nap and nap.

Comprehension Questions

"Ham and Yams"

1. What was in the pan?

2. What was in the bag?

3. What do Dad and Tad do with the ham and yams?

4. Who are the **characters** in this story?

5. Why do you think Dad and Tad have a nap?

6. What makes you need a nap?

7. Do you think Dad and Tad took a long nap? (Why or why not?)

"Max's Ham"

Max the Lab is sad.

Can Max have ham on the mat?

The ham is in the bag.

Max can have the ham in the bag.

Max wags for ham.

He wags for the ham in the bag.

Can Max have ham on the mat?

Max had ham on the mat.

He had ham on the tan mat.

Comprehension Questions 1-9b

"Max's Ham"

1. What did Max want?

2. How did he get what he wants?

3. Who is the **character** in this story?

4. Where is the **setting** of this story?

5. How did Max feel at the **beginning** of the story?

6. What did Max do at the **end** of the story?

"Jam in Dan's Van"

Sam	jam	I

Sam and I are pals.
I have jam for Sam.
Can Sam and I have jam in Dan's van?
Sam and I had jam in Dan's tan van.

They had jam on Dan's van.
The jam was on the van.

Dan is mad.
His van is bad.
Dan had to wax his tan van.
He had to wax his van.
Dan had to wax it with a rag.

Comprehension Questions

"Jam in Dan's Van"

1. What happened in Dan's van?

2. Why is Dan mad?

3. Who are the **characters** in this story?

4. Where is the **setting** of this story?

5. What did Dan have to do at the **end** of the story?

6. What would jam be like on a van?

7. What is **jam** in this story?
   a. stopped traffic
   b. a hurt finger
   c. jelly
   d. a tight spot

"Yams in a Bag"

Hal had a bag of yams.

Are the yams in the bag?

The yams are in the bag.

Can Sam and I have yams?

Sam and Hal had yams.

They sat and had yams in the pan.

They had yams in the pan with jam.

Sam and Hal had a bag of yams.

Comprehension Questions 1-9d

"Yams in a Bag"

1. What did Hal have?

2. Where are the yams?

3. Who wants the yams?

4. What were the yams in when Sal and Hal ate them?

5. They had yams in the pan with ___.

6. How many yams do you think Sam and Hal ate? Why?

7. What else might you eat with or on yams?

"Rags for Pam"

Pam	you

Pam ran to Sam's.

Sam is Pam's pal.

He had a bag of rags.

Sam had a bag of rags for Pam.

Sam had rags for Pam.

You can have the bag of rags, Pam.

Pam had the rags for Babs the cat.

Babs had rags for a mat.

Comprehension Questions 1-9e

"Rags for Pam"

1. Pam and Sam are ___.

2. What did Sam give to Pam?

3. What did Pam do with the rags?

4. What is the cat's name?

5. Who are the **characters** in this story?

6. How might you make a mat out of rags?

7. How do you think the mat felt?
   a. sticky
   b. slippery
   c. soft
   d. hard

"You Can Tag Pam"

I can tag Pam.
Pam ran and ran.
Can you tag Pam?
Pam can tag you.

You and I can tag Pam.
You can nab Pam.
Nab Pam!

Pam ran and ran.
Pam ran to the van.
Pam ran to the van to have a nap.
Pam had a nap in the van.

Comprehension Questions   1-9f

"You Can Tag Pam"

1. What game are the kids playing?

2. Who are the **characters** in this story?

3. Where do you think this story takes place? (What is the **setting**?) Why?

4. What does **nab** mean in this story?
   a. eat
   b. catch
   c. run
   d. a cracker

Review Words

cat	fat	pat	bat	rat
Dad	mad	Tad	tap	bag
nab	Max	pal	Dan	ran
jam	sat	tag	mat	rag
map	lap	hat	had	cap
sad	Pam	van	cab	gal
yam	Lab	wax	Hal	fan
bad	nap	pad	can	Sam
pal	ham	pan	Sal	man
Dad's	Tad's	Dan's	Hal's	

Review Sight Words

the	on	is	a	and
with	his	was	he	to
in	yellow	have	are	it
looks	they	I	you	

Made in the USA
Monee, IL
01 September 2022